3 9082 08628 7813

D1275443

O   12/04
O   9/08   ' To(89) 3.11 2010
                3.11/2010

ROYAL OAK PUBLIC LIBRARY
222 E. ELEVEN MILE ROAD
P.O. BOX 494
ROYAL OAK, MI 48068-0494
Library Hours
Monday 10-9
Tuesday 10-9
Wednesday 10-9
Thursday 10-9
Friday 10-6
Saturday 10-6

KEYSTONES

Muslim MOSQUE

Umar Hegedüs

Contents

A & C BLACK • LONDON

J
297
H
PUBLIC LIBRARY
FEB 13 2002
ROYAL OAK, MICH

Peace be with you

This book is about a mosque and about *Islam*, the way of peace. *Islam* is the way of life followed by Muslims throughout the world. Mosques are places of worship, assembly and learning. The children in this book visited the *Dar al-Islam* mosque in London. They wanted to find out what a mosque is like and discover what happens there.

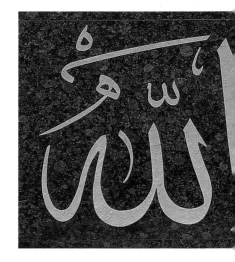

*Engraved into the granite wall ins. the mosque is the Arabic name for God. This is the first picture in the book, as Muslims believe that everything begins with **Allah**.*

Throughout this book you will see two Arabic symbols. The first ﷺ is made up of the words '*Salla-llahu alayhi wa salam*' — peace and blessings of *Allah* upon him. They are used by Muslims every time the Prophet Muhammad ﷺ is mentioned.

The second symbol ؑ is made up of the words '*Alayhi salam*' — peace be upon him. They are used by Muslims after the names of Prophets are mentioned. Many Muslims also say these words after mentioning any of the twelve *Imams* descended from the Prophet Muhammad ﷺ.

*The Arabic words 'Dar al-Islam' on the outside of the mosque mean 'Home of Peace'. The mosque was opened in 1993. The poem carved in Arabic inside the mosque begins: 'This is a house built for the love of **Allah** and for the protection of people'.*

Everyone who visits the Dar al-Islam mosque is welcomed with the traditional Islamic greeting *'As-Salamu alaykum'*, which means 'peace be with you'. The Imam in charge of the mosque, is called Sayyid Husayn Baraka. The title *Sayyid* means that he is a descendant of the Prophet Muhammad ﷺ.

The final message of Islam was brought to people everywhere by the Prophet Muhammad ﷺ. That message teaches that there is no god except Allah, the Creator of everyone and everything.

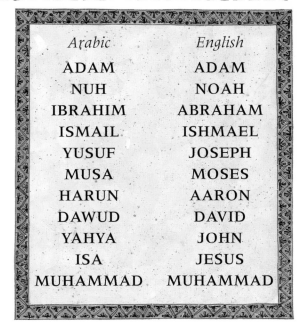

Arabic	English
ADAM	ADAM
NUH	NOAH
IBRAHIM	ABRAHAM
ISMAIL	ISHMAEL
YUSUF	JOSEPH
MUSA	MOSES
HARUN	AARON
DAWUD	DAVID
YAHYA	JOHN
ISA	JESUS
MUHAMMAD	MUHAMMAD

Allah chose especially good people to show how He wants everyone to be. These special people are His Prophets and Messengers. They were sent to every nation and tribe on earth with the same good news. Many people all over the world are named after them.

Sayyid Husayn Baraka explained to the children that Islam teaches people to live in peace and harmony with everyone and everything. People of every race can choose to be Muslim. A person becomes a Muslim by declaring their faith in Islam and saying the *Shahadah*: 'I testify that there is no god except *Allah* and I testify that Muhammad is the Messenger of *Allah*.'

Muslims live an Islamic life by praying regularly, giving to charity, going on pilgrimage and fasting during *Ramadan*. They believe that on the last day, everyone will have to answer to *Allah* for the way they have lived.

Sayyid Husayn Baraka, his sons Musa and Jafar, and their schoolfriend Fereshteh welcome Hannah and Didi with greetings of 'Peace'.

The world is a mosque

Before the children went into the prayer hall of the mosque, they took off their shoes. The first thing they noticed was the beautifully tiled *mihrab*. This is the alcove which shows the direction of Makkah, a city in Arabia. Wherever Muslims may be in the world, north, south, east or west, they always face towards the *Ka'bah* in Makkah when they worship *Allah*.

The children noticed that there was no furniture in the prayer hall, which made it seem very spacious.

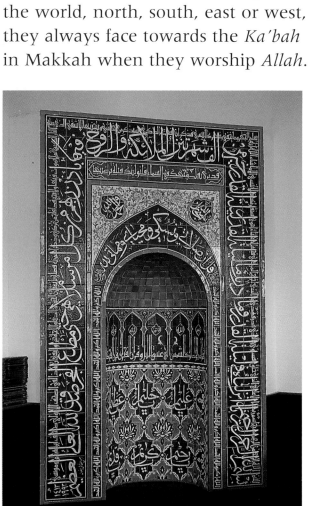

Over four thousand years ago the *Ka'bah* was built by the Prophet Ibrahim ﷺ and his son Ismail ﷺ for the worship of *Allah*, the Arabic name for God. The Prophet Muhammad ﷺ, was born in Makkah and was a descendant of the Prophet Ibrahim ﷺ. He too faced the *Ka'bah* to pray to the 'One True God'. Sayyid Husayn Baraka explained to the children that Muslims offer *Salah* (prayers) five times a day when they ask *Allah* to guide them.

*The **mihrab**, the niche or alcove in the mosque wall, indicates the '**qiblah**', the direction of the **Ka'bah**. The **mihrab** is made from beautifully patterned tiles. They were hand-made in Iran especially for this mosque.*

During *Salah*, Muslims stand, bow and kneel with their foreheads on the floor. Now the children understood why everyone has to take their shoes off in the prayer hall. That way the mosque carpet is kept clean enough to pray on.

Fereshteh told the others that Muslims don't only pray when they are in a mosque. She said that she prays at home with her family and at her school there is a room specially to pray in. When her family and friends go on picnics in the summer, they pray outside.

*Fereshteh pointed out the words, 'And from Him (Allah) we seek help' written in Arabic on the **mihrab**.*

*In the sacred mosque in Makkah, Muslims pray surrounding and facing the **Ka'bah**.*

Sayyid Husayn Baraka told the children that he enjoyed praying in the fresh air and that the Prophet Muhammad ﷺ said,

'All of the earth is a mosque' (**Hadith**: Sahih al-Bukhari — The Chapter of Prophets' tradition number 3172)

Because the whole world can be a place of worship, Muslims are taught to treat every part of it with respect and care.

The Prophet's Mosque

The children wanted to know if all mosques look the same inside. To explain, Sayyid Husayn Baraka told them about the Prophet Muhammad's mosque.

By the year 622 CE the good news of Islam had spread across Arabia. The Prophet Muhammad ﷺ was teaching people what Allah had revealed to him — that everyone should live in peace with one another. When the people of Yathrib heard this they wanted the fighting among their different clans to stop. They invited the Prophet Muhammad ﷺ and his followers to live there. They wanted the Prophet ﷺ to become the leader and to make peace between the clans.

Everyone in Yathrib wanted the honour of looking after the Prophet ﷺ. He did not want to say no to any of them. So he let his camel wander through the town until it found a place to rest. There he built a small mud brick house. Like all the others in Yathrib it had a roof of palm leaves and faced into a courtyard.

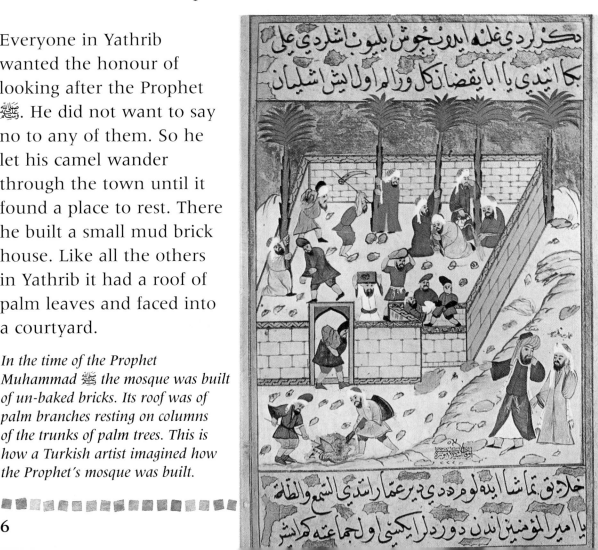

In the time of the Prophet Muhammad ﷺ the mosque was built of un-baked bricks. Its roof was of palm branches resting on columns of the trunks of palm trees. This is how a Turkish artist imagined how the Prophet's mosque was built.

Every day crowds came to pray in the courtyard of the Prophet's house. They often stayed to listen to him speak, and ask for his advice and his help to settle differences between them. The Prophet ﷺ gave them a fair system of laws and the clans promised to help one another in times of trouble. From that time on, Yathrib became known as Madinah-un-Nabi, the City of the Prophet. But most people just say Madinah.

Doing things the way the Prophet ﷺ did, is called following the *Sunnah* of the Prophet ﷺ. The Prophet's followers told their friends and families what they had seen him do and what they had heard him say. Many of these reports were carefully checked and collected. They are called the *Hadith*. Muslims study *Hadith* to learn how to live a good Islamic life.

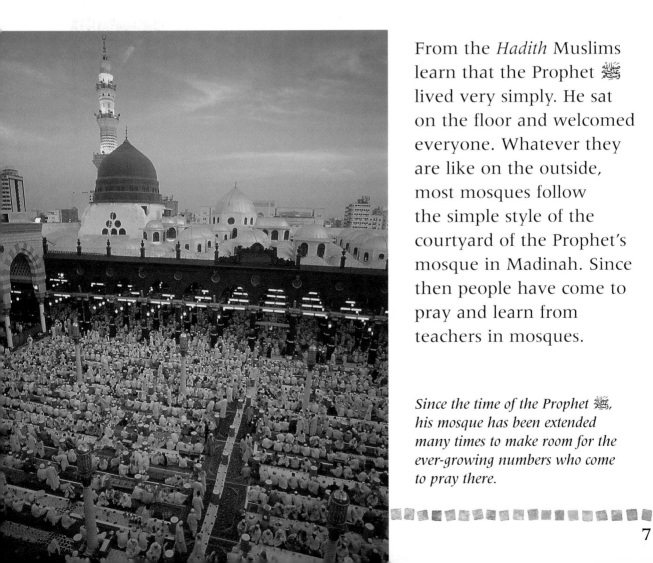

From the *Hadith* Muslims learn that the Prophet ﷺ lived very simply. He sat on the floor and welcomed everyone. Whatever they are like on the outside, most mosques follow the simple style of the courtyard of the Prophet's mosque in Madinah. Since then people have come to pray and learn from teachers in mosques.

Since the time of the Prophet ﷺ, his mosque has been extended many times to make room for the ever-growing numbers who come to pray there.

In the prayer hall

The children explored the main prayer hall. They noticed the beautiful crystal lights which hang from the ceiling. The floor is covered with a specially woven carpet to pray on.

The colour green was chosen because it was the Prophet Muhammad's favourite colour. The white design in the carpet marks out enough space for each person to pray on.

*Musa pointed out that the arch shapes point in the direction of the **Ka'bah** in Makkah, just like the **mihrab**.*

IMAM ALI BIN ABI TALIB

"The true worth of every individual is in what he does best".

Around the walls of the mosque are twelve smaller granite slabs. These give the names of some of the Prophet Muhammad's family. Some of the good words they said are also written on the slabs.

After the Prophet Muhammad ﷺ passed away, his cousin and son-in-law Ali ؓ and after him, the Prophet's grandsons (may Allah grant them all peace) made sure that no-one forgot the example and teachings of the Prophet ﷺ. They in their turn passed this responsibility to their descendants.

These twelve very special, wise and good people are called the *Imams*. Wherever they were, they led their Islamic community on the straight path and continued to keep the *Sunnah* of the Prophet ﷺ alive by teaching as many people as they could.

*This old Islamic painting shows a teacher giving a talk from the **minbar**.*

At one end of the mosque there is a short set of stairs, called the *minbar*, which doesn't seem to go anywhere. Like the carpet, the *minbar's* wooden sides have a geometric pattern. Near the top of the stairs is a microphone. The children wondered what the stairs were for. Musa explained that when Sayyid Husayn Baraka is talking to the people, he sits on the stairs so that everyone can see and hear him.

*This simply designed **minbar** is where the **Imam** sits when he gives a talk.*

The City of Knowledge

The first words of the *Qur'an* which were revealed to the Prophet Muhammad ﷺ are, 'Read in the name of your Lord'. These words teach Muslims how important it is to read, write and learn. Ever since the Prophet Muhammad ﷺ first taught Allah's message, mosques have been places of teaching and learning.

*The **Qur'an** rest is useful for people who read and study the **Qur'an** for long periods of time.*

People always ask, 'Why this ?', or, 'Why that?' And there was no better place than the mosque for them to find someone to sort out a problem or to explain something. Among the Prophet's most faithful followers was his cousin and son-in-law Ali ﷺ. The Prophet ﷺ called Ali ﷺ 'The Gate to the City of Knowledge'. People flocked to consult Ali ﷺ at his mosque in Kufah in Iraq, where he passed on what the Prophet ﷺ had taught him. No one could match his knowledge of Islam, Arabic Grammar, Science and Law.

As Islam spread, new mosques were built with *madrasahs* (schools or colleges) attached to them. Young children learned to read, write and study the *Qur'an*. Lessons for older students included subjects such as mathematics, science, geography and logic.

At the Dar al-Islam school the older girls study the lives and work of famous Muslim scholars.

At these early 'teaching circles', pupils sat at the feet of 'learned masters' and studied all branches of Islamic knowledge. The world's first universities developed from these circles.

The teaching circles in mosques encouraged Muslims to look at the natural world, and to study such things as the growth of plants, the movement of the planets, and the cycle of the seasons.

The children learned that many of the things we take for granted, such as the use of zero in mathematics, studies of eclipses in astronomy, and knowledge of diseases such as meningitis and tuberculosis, were developed by Islamic scholars.

▲ *The astrolabe, which helped sailors to find their position at sea, was invented by a Muslim scholar hundreds of years ago.*

◄ *In a mosque in Palestine, young boys discuss the meaning of the **Qur'an** with their teacher.*

Helping others

Sayyid Husayn Baraka introduced the children to people in the mosque who are working to help the community. Almost everyone who works at the mosque gives their time without pay. They want to help others and make the mosque a useful centre.

The library is an important part of the mosque. It provides a quiet study area where people may come to read or to prepare for their exams. There are beautiful old *Qur'ans* and books on poetry, history and Islamic law. The librarian orders new books and makes sure that information is easy to find.

The librarian showed the children some books about Islam.

When children are just four years old they start to come to Saturday school at the mosque. They learn about Islam and how to read and write in the Arabic language. They are taught to memorise the *Qur'an*. They begin with short passages. As they grow older, some of them will learn the whole *Qur'an* by heart.

*These boys at the Dar al-Islam **madrasah** are studying the **Qur'an**.*

*While the children in this book were visiting the mosque, the pupils at the **madrasah** had their school photograph taken. Can you spot Fereshteh and Musa in the picture?*

Muslims try to help those who are less fortunate. Donations came from all over the world to support this Muslim-run orphanage in Hebron in Palestine.

The children met the people from the mosque who have been chosen to look after the welfare of their community. They were interested to learn that Islam developed the world's very first welfare state. By this system, the whole community shares in helping people in need.

After meeting their yearly expenses, Muslims have to pay a share of the money they have left into a community fund. This is called *Zakah*. The money and goods that are collected are shared out to help those in need.

Many Muslims give much more than *Zakah*. They also contribute *Khums*, which is a fifth of the money they have left over from what they have earned each year. Even if they have no money, all Muslims can give *Sadaqah*, which means any good or charitable act.

The Muslim day

Suddenly the *Adhan*, the call to prayer, resounds throughout the mosque. The children heard the *Mu'adhin* call to everyone in a powerful voice, 'Come to prayer, come to success'. The pupils leave the *madrasah*, and the people reading in the library put down their books. Everyone knows that it is time for *Salah*, time to worship *Allah*. Sayyid Husayn Baraka explained to the children that the five daily times of *Salah* are fixed by *Allah* in the *Qur'an*. (Surah 30:17-18)

THE FIVE DAILY TIMES FOR *SALAH*

Salat-ul-Fajr is offered between the first light of dawn and sunrise.

Salat-ul-Zuhr is offered after midday.

Salat-ul-Asr is offered in the mid afternoon.

Salat-ul-Maghrib, the sunset prayer also marks the time for breaking fast during the month of Ramadan.

Salat-ul-Isha is offered from about an hour and a half after *Salat-ul-Maghrib*.

The children watched as everyone from the *madrasah*, office, library and kitchen gathered in the prayer hall. They were joined by people who had arrived at the mosque in time to offer their *Salah*. Muslims believe that praying together in a group brings greater blessings than praying alone. Sayyid Husayn Baraka explained to the children that the Prophet ﷺ said,

'Prayer at home is counted once, prayer at the local mosque is equivalent to twenty five prayers'.
(**Hadith:** Sunan ibn Majah — Book of Mosques and Congregations tradition number 1403)

As everyone prepared for **Salah***, Musa showed the others how Muslims make* **wudu***, or wash before prayer. He explained that Allah tells us in the* **Qur'an***:*

O you who believe! When you prepare for prayer, wash your faces, and your hands and arms to the elbows; wipe your heads with water; and wash your feet to the ankles.
Qur'an 5:6

During Salah, everyone stands in long straight rows behind the Imam. The men and boys stand together, the women and girls together make their own rows. The Imam calls out the words Allahu Akbar — Allah is Most Great and then recites a part of the Qur'an. Everyone follows him as he stands, bows and kneels with his forehead touching the ground. They too bow and kneel with respect to Allah.

The children could see how Salah is the way in which Muslims communicate with and worship their Creator. Afterwards the Imam explained that, just as bodies need food, souls need the nourishment of Salah, and that people are refreshed by their 'prayer break'.

▲ During **Salah** everyone stands in rows behind the **Imam**.

▲ The girls too, follow just what the **Imam** does.

The highlight of the week

The children learned that, for Muslims, Friday is the most important day of the week, as it is the day of Assembly. Shortly after midday, crowds of men, women and children gather in the mosque to listen to the *Imam's* talk.

Everything is done just as the Prophet Muhammad ﷺ did in his mosque in Madinah. In the Prophet's Friday talk he taught how *Allah* wants people to behave. He reminded them to believe in the one and only Creator. He advised them on how to deal with the problems of everyday life. Afterwards, everyone had the chance to meet and talk.

These meetings are still important for Muslim communities, particularly in countries where there are few Muslims. By attending *Salat-ul-Jumu'ah*, the Friday prayer, people can get to know one another and give each other support during difficult times.

The Prophet ﷺ said,

Prayer in a mosque in which **Jumu'ah Salat** prayer is celebrated is equivalent to five hundred prayers.

(**Hadith**: Sunan ibn Majah)

The need to attend *Salat-ul-Jumu'ah* is one of the main reasons why Muslims work so hard to build mosques wherever they live. Some communities start by holding the Friday prayer in someone's home or office, or in a rented hall. The members of a Muslim community may save whatever they can to buy or build a place big enough for everyone to pray in. There are specially built mosques in almost every country (look at the time-line on pages 28 and 29).

◄ *This **Qur'an** has been written out so beautifully by hand to show respect and love for Allah's divine words.*

▲ *Sayyid Husayn Baraka sits on the **minbar** so that everyone in the prayer hall can see him and hear his talk.*

◄ *Every Friday after midday, the mosque gets very crowded for **Salat-ul-Jumu'ah**.*

The heart of the community

It is the social and religious duty of Muslims to care for everyone within their neighbourhood, whether or not their neighbours are Muslim. A neighbour is anyone who lives within forty houses in any direction. The mosque is the focus of Muslim community life. The Arabic name for the congregation of people who pray together and use the same mosque is the *Jammah*.

A mosque can be a busy place on any day of the week. The children looked at the rota for the groups, events and people who use the *Dar al-Islam* mosque as their community centre. They saw that every morning mothers run a toddlers' play group. At midday, retired people meet together for lunch. In the evenings, younger people can take part in a variety of sporting and drama activities as well as studying Islam and doing charitable work.

A 'drop in' advice service is provided at the mosque. If the advisors are not able to solve someone's problem themselves, they usually know someone who can.

So many local school teachers have asked for information about Islam, that the mosque has set up a resource centre. Schools are welcome to bring classes to the mosque and pupils as well as the mosque's community enjoy these visits.

On three afternoons during the week, advice sessions are held at the mosque.

Families sometimes use the mosque's meeting halls to celebrate a wedding or the birth of a baby. A Muslim wedding can be conducted anywhere as long as two male witnesses are present. A meal is served to the whole community to celebrate the good news of a marriage. Everyone prays for the couple's future happiness.

This father is whispering the call to prayer ▶ *into the right ear of his newborn baby.*

During this wedding, the Bride and Groom sat in separate parts of the mosque and took it in turns to agree to the marriage contract.

When someone in the community dies, they are taken in a coffin to the mosque. There the *Janazah*, the funeral prayer, is recited for their soul and some good words are said about their life. Over the next few days and weeks, people from the *Jammah* will comfort and support the bereaved family by reading the *Qur'an* both at the family's home and at the mosque.

The Islamic year

In the library, Musa showed the children an Islamic calendar. He told them that the Islamic dating system began over fourteen hundred years ago when the Prophet Muhammad ﷺ moved to Madinah. The Islamic year is based on the moon's cycle. A new month begins at the time of every new moon. Since a lunar month is 29.5 days long, a lunar year lasts for 354 days. This is eleven days shorter than the January to December calendar. This means that each of the days Muslims remember in the Islamic calendar will, over the years, fall in all of the seasons of spring, summer, autumn or winter in turn.

MONTH	DATE	OCCASION
Muharram	1	Hijrah — Migration (in the year 622 CE). The Prophet ﷺ moves to Madinah to establish the first Islamic State. Islamic new year.
	10	Ashura (680 CE). The martyrdom of the Prophet's grandson Imam Husayn ﷺ at Kerbala in Iraq. People retell the history of events with sorrow.
Safar	3	The Birthday of Muhammad al-Baqir ﷺ the fifth Imam. (675 CE).
	7	The Birthday of Musa al-Kazim ﷺ the seventh Imam (744 CE).
Rabi' al-Awwal	12–17	Maulid an-Nabi (570 CE). Commemorates the birth, life and example of Muhammad ﷺ. This week is used to promote Islamic unity and awareness of the Prophet's life and work and give thanks to Allah.
	17	The Birthday of Jafar al-Sadiq ﷺ the sixth Imam (702 CE).
Rabi' al-Thani	8	The Birthday of al-Hasan al-Askeri ﷺ the eleventh Imam (845 CE).
Jumada al-Awwal		

MONTH	DATE	OCCASION
Jumada al-Thani	20	The Birthday of Fatimah Zahrah ﷺ (615 CE). The beloved daughter of the Prophet Muhammad ﷺ, wife of the First Imam and mother of Hasan and Husayn ﷺ. She is known as the leader of women.
Rajab	2	The birthday of Ali- al-Naqi ﷺ the tenth Imam (827 CE).
	10	The birthday of Muhammad al-Taqi ﷺ the ninth Imam (809 CE).
	13	The birthday of Ali ibn Abu-Talib ﷺ the first Imam (600 CE).
	27	Laylat ul-Isra wal Mi'raj Commemorates the night journey and ascent of the Prophet Muhammad ﷺ from Makkah to Jerusalem and through the seven heavens where he received *Allah's* instructions about *Salah*. People offer extra prayers.
	27	Id ul-Mabath 610 CE Commemorates the start of the prophetic work of the Prophet Muhammad ﷺ. People offer extra prayers and read the *Qur'an*.

Allah has ordered Muslims to commemorate *Ramadan* and *Id ul-Fitr*, *Hajj* and *Id ul-Adha*. Many also remember the birthdays of the Prophet ﷺ and his family. On such occasions people gather in mosques to pray for them and retell stories about their lives. Historians differ on the dates, but those shown below have been agreed upon by most of the Prophet's family.

The children looked at an Islamic calendar which showed them the phases of the moon.

MONTH	DATE	OCCASION
Sha'ban	3	The birthday of Al-Husayn ibn Ali ﷺ the third Imam (626 CE).
	5	The Birthday of Zayn al-Abidin ﷺ the fourth Imam (659 CE).
	14	Laylat ul-Barat The night of promises when Allah decides what will happen to all of His creation in the coming year. People pray for forgiveness.
	15	The birthday of Muhammad al-Mahdi ﷺ the twelfth Imam (868 CE).
Ramadan	The month of fasting	People fast from food and water from before dawn to sunset on each day of this month. As ordered by *Allah* in the *Qur'an*, this gives a special sense of community. (Ref. *Qur'an* 2:183).
	15	The birthday of al-Hasan al-Mujtaba ﷺ the second Imam (625 CE).
	19–29	Laylat ul-Qadr This blessed night falls on one of the last ten nights of *Ramadan*. It commemorates the revelation of the *Qur'an* to the Prophet Muhammad ﷺ. (Ref. *Qur'an* 97).

MONTH	DATE	OCCASION
Shawwal	1	Id ul-Fitr This festival marks the start of the new month and the end of fasting. People attend *Id Salah* at the mosque and give *Zakat-ul-Fitr* to ensure every one can join the festivities.
Dhul Qad'ah	11	The Birthday of Ali al-Rida ﷺ the eighth Imam (765 CE).
Dhul Hijjah	8–10	The Hajj – Pilgrimage to Makkah Commemorates events in the life of the Prophets Ibrahim, Ismail and Muhammad (peace and blessings upon them all) as ordered in the *Qur'an*. Muslims must make the *Hajj* at least once in their life.
	10	Id ul-Adha The feast of Sacrifice which is part of the *Hajj*. People attend *Id Salah* at the mosque.
	18	Id ul-Ghadir (632 CE). Commemorates when, after the Prophet's last *Hajj* he told the people that Ali ﷺ was his successor. (*Hadith*: Tirmidhi & Hanbal)

Ramadan and Id-ul-Fitr

The month of *Ramadan* is a very special time for Muslims everywhere. It is the ninth month of the Islamic calendar and the month in which *Allah* Almighty chose to send down His *Qur'an* 'as a guidance to people'. Musa told the children that Muslims know that the month of *Ramadan* has started when they see the new moon. For every one of the next twenty nine or thirty days, Muslims everywhere fast from just before dawn until sunset, as ordered by *Allah* in the *Qur'an*.

Fasting doesn't just mean not eating or drinking. When people fast, they try extra hard to be and do good. Lots of people spend more time reading and studying the *Qur'an* and less time watching television and chatting to their friends.

Fasting is sometimes difficult because everyone gets hungry and thirsty. It helps to know that Muslims in every part of the world are doing the same thing.

Fereshteh told the children that part of the fun of *Ramadan* is going to the mosque at night where everyone breaks their fast together.

On special nights huge pots of rice are cooked in the kitchen at Dar al-Islam mosque so that people can break their fast together.

Plastics table cloths are spread over the carpet and everyone eats 'picnic style'.

On one special night, Laylat ul-Qadr, everyone makes an even greater effort to visit the mosque and pray for *Allah's* mercy and blessings.

Just as people share food during this holy month, they also give money so that everyone can prepare to celebrate the *Id*, when the new moon is seen and the month of *Ramadan* is over.

The first day of the new month of *Shawwal* is *Id ul-Fitr*. Musa and Fereshteh described to the others how exiting it is for them to get up early and go to the mosque in their best clothes.

After the *Id Salah*, the children are given fruit and sweets. Musa says it feels funny to be eating during the day, but he's happy to have been able to complete all the days of fasting.

Friends having fun on the day of the Id. ▶

Hajj and Id-ul-Adha

Musa told the children that every year during the month of *Hajj* some of the people from Dar al-Islam mosque go on pilgrimage. *Hajj* is the annual pilgrimage to Makkah in Arabia which each adult Muslim must make at least once in their lifetime. People are only expected to go if they are well and can afford it.

Five times, every day of their lives, Muslims turn towards the *Ka'bah* for *Salah*. So it's easy to imagine how wonderful it must be for them to visit the *Ka'bah* as part of the *Hajj*. People on *Hajj* follow in the footsteps and re-live some of the actions of the Prophets Ibrahim, Ismail and Muhammad (may Allah grant them all His peace and blessings).

These tents shelter people from the blistering sun on the day they spend at Arafat during the Hajj.

In the year 632 CE. when the Prophet Muhammad ﷺ made the last pilgrimage of his lifetime, over seventy thousand people travelled with him. Nowadays as many as two million people, of every race and colour, from all over the world, come together each year at *Hajj* time.

Pilgrims may stay in Arabia for two to three weeks and visit the Prophet's Mosque in Madinah. The events of the *Hajj* itself take place over a few special days.

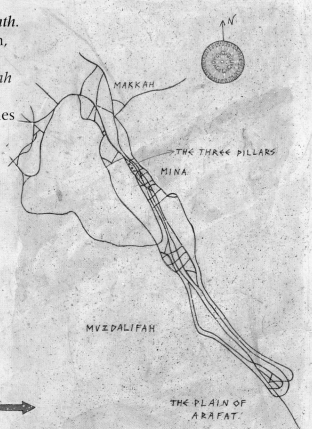

By day eight of the Hajj month. In the mosque in Makkah, pilgrims make *tawaf* by walking around the *Ka'bah* seven times. They make *sa'y* by walking seven times between two hills in the footsteps of the Prophet Ibrahim's wife. Stay overnight at Mina.

Day nine of the Hajj month. Pilgrims spend the day praying for forgiveness at Arafat where the Prophet spoke to everyone on his last pilgrimage. At sunset they go to Muzdalifah to collect small pebbles. After sunrise they leave for Mina.

Days 11, 12 and 13 Pilgrims stay in Mina for at least two days. They throw pebbles at all three pillars each day. They go to Makkah to make a farewell *tawaf* of the *Ka'bah*.

Day ten – Id ul-Adha At Mina, pilgrims throw pebbles at the biggest pillars representing the devil. They may sacrifice an animal. They go to Makkah and make *tawaf* and return to Mina.

*Both the men's and women's sections of this mosque are packed for the **Id Salah**.*

On *Id-ul-Adha*, the festival of sacrifice, Muslims everywhere, even those who are not on *Hajj* attend a special *Id Salah*. On that day, they are reminded of Prophet Ibrahim's readiness to obey *Allah* in everything. They thank *Allah* that so many different people of every nationality, meet peacefully together during *Hajj* to form one *Ummah*, a vast community of believers. Everyone prays that one day all of *Allah's* creatures will live together in peace and treat each other justly.

Allah's creation

The children have learned how the *Qur'an* plays an important part in the lives of Muslims. But, Fereshteh tells them, that's not all Muslims learn from the *Qur'an*. It is sometimes described as, 'the book of signs for people who think.' Everything in the natural world is seen as a sign of the Creator.

It is We who send down rain from the skies: with it We produce vegetation of all kinds . . .

Qur'an 6:99

The Muslims at the Dar al-Islam mosque like to make sure the birds have enough to eat in winter.

For hundreds of years, flowers have been an important feature of Islamic art.

Fereshteh told the children that even though there is only a little garden at the mosque, everyone likes to help look after it. Plants are chosen to attract insects, butterflies and birds.

Muslims believe that *Allah* has created everything in the universe and that everything in Creation is linked and interdependent.

They also believe that He made human beings the caretakers of the world and they feel honoured to have been given this responsibility. Muslims learn from *Allah* and the Prophet Muhammad ﷺ that the creatures, plants and minerals of the earth must be cared for and used wisely.

The profits from the sale of the olives in this Palestinian grove are used for the education of children who could not otherwise afford to go to school.

This means that people may not spoil, waste or destroy anything in or on the earth, sea or sky. Whenever they can, they should use renewable sources of energy, such as solar, wind and water power. Sayyid Husayn Baraka told the children that *Allah* tells us in the *Qur'an* that we should

'live on what He provides but always bear in mind that you will all one day be answerable to *Allah*.' (*Qur'an* 67:15)

Time-line

Since the Prophet Ibrahim ﷺ built the *Ka'bah*, the *Bayt Allah* or
the House of *Allah*, people all over the world have made houses
to worship in. Down the centuries Islam as a way of peace has
spread throughout the world. Wherever and whenever the Islamic
way of life flourished, Muslims on every continent built mosques as
the heart of their communities. On the outside, mosques often look
just like the other buildings around them. But on the inside, they
all have a large open area to pray in.

THE KUDUS MINARET

Early 1500 CE

Large numbers of Javanese become
Muslim. They built at Kudus, a red
brick minaret, the tower from which
people are called to prayer. It is built
in the same style as traditional
Javanese Hindu temples.

1442 CE

The Aidkah mosque is built in the central
square of Kashgar, in China. On Fridays
up to 10, 000 people come from miles
around to pray. The wooden ceiling of
the prayer hall is held up by 140 carved
pillars. For a thousand years, Chinese
Muslims have lived in peace.

1569 – 75 CE

The Selimiye
Mosque in
Turkey is built.
It has four
slender minarets,
each over
70 meters tall.

THE FRIDAY
MOSQUE

THE HAYMARKET MOSQUE

1612-1637 CE

The Royal Mosque is built
in Isfahan, in Iran. It is
covered with tile mosaic on
the outside. Its beautiful
dome is reflected in the
pool at the centre of
the courtyard.

Late 1700 CE

The Friday Mosque is
built in Namu, in
Guinea. It is an amazing
circular building, which
is thatched to make
the frequent rain run
off quickly.

1849 CE

The Haymarket mosque
is built in Kazan, a city
on the Volga River in
Russia. The people in
that area accepted Islam
as their way of life in
922 CE.

28

2,000 BCE

The Ka'bah is built as a simple cube-shaped building made from big blocks of stone.

622 CE

Year one of the Islamic 'Hijri' calendar. The Prophet's Mosque in Madinah was built next to the home of the Prophet Muhammad ﷺ.

632 CE

The final Prophet ﷺ dies in Madinah.

680 CE

The Prophet's grandson Imam Husayn ﷺ and seventy followers are murdered defending Islam.

THE KA'BAH

THE GREAT MOSQUE OF CORDOBA

690 – 692 CE

The Dome of the Rock is built in Jerusalem, Palestine. It is a special place for Muslims because the Prophet Muhammad ﷺ ascended through the seven heavens from the rock.

1398 CE

The Friday Mosque in Srinagar, Kashmir is built. It is carved out of wood from nearby forests.

970 – 972 CE

The al-Azhar mosque is built in Cairo, in Egypt. It becomes a place of study for students of Islam.

784 – 786 CE

The Great Mosque of Cordoba in Spain is built. It is famous for its beautiful arches.

THE DOME OF THE ROCK

1894 CE

The first purpose-built mosque in Britain is completed at Woking, in Surrey.

1993 CE

The Great Mosque of Casablanca in Morocco is opened. It is one of the largest mosques in the world – 100,000 people can pray together at the same time. Its pink marble walls can be seen from thirty km away. A beam of laser light shines out from the 230m minaret for twenty five km showing the direction of Makkah.

The Dar al-Islam mosque is opened in London.

1996 CE

Prince Charles visits the newly built Borah Mosque in Northolt, in West London. It has a sports hall and a kitchen which can feed a thousand people at a time.

29

How to find out more

Visiting a mosque

On a visit to a purpose-built mosque or building fully converted for use as an Islamic centre and place of worship, look out for these features:

The mihrab — a niche or alcove in the mosque wall which indicates the 'Qiblah' — the direction of the *Ka'bah* in Makkah

The minbar — a platform in the mosque from which the Imam delivers his talk.

Madrasah — a place of study within the mosque.

Arabic calligraphy — beautifully written and specially chosen sections of the *Qur'an*.

Sadaqah box — for people to make charitable donations.

Shoe racks — to store everyone's shoes tidily and make them easy to find.

If you are going to walk inside the prayer hall, you will need to take off your shoes first; clean socks are obviously important. To respect Islamic views on modesty, women and girls should wear headscarves, long-sleeved tops and loose trousers or longer skirts.

No one should ever walk in front of a Muslim who is praying. Always ask permission before taking photographs of the features at the mosque and check first to make sure that anyone you want to photograph is happy to have their picture taken.

It is an Islamic tradition to offer hospitality to guests whether at home or at the mosque. Visitors are sometimes invited to eat or are given refreshments in a dining area. Food and drink should not otherwise be taken into the mosque.

Arranging a visit

When organising a group visit to a mosque, give as much notice as you can, to enable the Muslim community to ensure that a knowledgeable person is available to talk to interested visitors.

There are more than a thousand mosques in Britain. If you do not know the location of your nearest mosque, the local SACRE (the LEA's Standing Advisory Committee for Religious Education) may be able to help. The Clerk to SACRE will often have a list of nearby places of worship for all the major faiths. Enjoy your visit!

A rack to keep shoes tidy at the mosque.

Useful words

Adhan The call to prayer.
Allah The Islamic name for the One True God in the Arabic language.
Hadith The sayings of the Prophet Muhammad ﷺ.
Hajj The annual pilgrimage to Makkah, which each Muslim must make at least once if he or she is healthy and has enough money.
Hijri The Islamic calendar which starts from the Hijrah — the year of the Prophet Muhammad's move from Makkah to Madinah.
Id A religious holiday, a day of celebration. Id-ul-Adha is celebrated during the Hajj; Id-ul-Fitr marks the end of Ramadan.
Imam A person who leads others in prayer. It is the title given to the members of the Prophet Muhammad's family who continued his teachings. The founder of an Islamic school of law is also called Imam.
Islam The inner peace which comes to people who are happy to obey Allah's loving guidance.

Jammah A community of Muslims who pray together.
Janazah The funeral prayer, recited for the soul of someone who has died.
Ka'bah The cube-shaped building in the centre of the grand mosque in Makkah, the first house built for the worship of the One True God.
Khums A donation to help the community of one fifth of what is left over from someone's yearly income.
Minbar The platform in a mosque from which the Imam gives his talk.
Mu'adhin The person who calls people to prayer.
Prophet A Messenger sent from Allah to bring good news and warn humankind.
Qur'an The Divine Book revealed to Prophet Muhammad ﷺ.
Ramadan The ninth month of the Islamic calendar during which Muslims fast from before dawn until sunset.
Sadaqah A good action or a willing gift to charity.
Salah Worshipping and praying to Allah, in the way taught by the Prophet

Muhammad ﷺ. The prayers are recited in the Arabic.
Sa'y Walking seven times between two hills at Makkah, as part of the Hajj, in memory of the Prophet Ibrahim's wife's search for water.
Sayyid A title of respect given to descendants of the Prophet Muhammad ﷺ through his daughter Fatimah ﷺ and her husband Ali ﷺ.
Shahadah The declaration of faith in Allah and His Messenger.
Sunnah The custom, tradition and example of the Prophet Muhammad ﷺ.
Tawaf Walking seven times around the Ka'bah in worship of Allah.
Ummah The world-wide community of Muslims.
Zakah A yearly purifying share of wealth paid to help the community.

3 9082 08628 7813

Index

First paperback edition 2000

First published 1997 in hardback by
A & C Black (Publishers) Ltd
35 Bedford Row
London WC1R 4JH

ISBN 0-7136-5344-2

Books in the Keystones series
available in hardback:
Buddhist Vihara
Christian Church
Hindu Mandir
Sikh Gurdwara
© 1997 A & C Black (Publishers) Ltd

A CIP catalogue record for this book is available
from the British Library

For the sake of what *Allah* tells us in the *Qur'an*:
O people. We created you from a single pair of a
male and a female, And made you into nations
and tribes, that you may know each other.
(Not that you may despise each other)
Qur'an 49:13

Umar Hegedüs asserts his right to be identified as
the author of this work, in accordance with the
Copyright Designs and Patents Act 1988

All transliterations and definitions of Islamic terms
correspond to those used in most LEA syllabuses
for religious education.

Acknowledgements
The author and publisher would like to thank the
following people for their help with this book:
Sayyid Fadhel Milani and Dr Muhammad
Movahedi; Sayyid Husayn Baraka the Jammah and
children of Dar-al-Islam mosque and madrasah;
Dhia Owainati, architect of Dar al-Islam mosque;
Fereshteh, Sayyid Musa, Hannah and Didi and
their headteachers, Mrs Davies and Mrs Kazmi;
The Amana Trust; ICES (Islamic Consultancy and
Education Service) PO Box 2842 London W6 9ZH;
Tayyeb Shah and Lubna Hussain; Benjamin and Ali
Dunn and family. All photographs by Jak Kilby
(Muhsin Abdullah)except for: pp 4a, 9b, Dhia
Owainati; p7 Peter Sanders; p11 Bridgeman Art
Library; pp10a, 16b, 17a, 26a, Umar Hegedüs;
p11b, 24 TRIP Photo Library.

All artwork by Vanessa Card

All rights reserved. No part of this publication
may be reproduced in any form or by any
means – graphic, electronic or mechanical,
including photocopying, recording, taping or
information storage and retrieval systems –
without the prior permission in writing of
the publishers.

Printed in Hong Kong
by Wing King Tong Co. Ltd